MW00329360

SUBLIME
CONFINEMENT

Copyright © Gary W. Ross 2017

All rights reserved. Printed in the United States of America.
No part of this book may be reproduced or transmitted in any form
or by any means, electronic or mechanical, including photocopying,
recording, or by any information storage and retrieval systems,
except in brief extracts for the purpose of review, without the written
permission of the author.

CATALOGING DATA:
Sublime Confinement
By Gary W. Ross

ISBN: 978-0-9986615-8-2

Cover design, interior design: Jim Shubin, Book Alchemist
www.bookalchemist.net

SUBLIME CONFINEMENT

To THE WONDERFUL
SARAH + BORIS

Gary W. Ross

TEA LEAF PUBLISHING

FORWORD

When I left Wall Street in 2004, after an exciting and rewarding 35 year career, I had no plans for my future. I just needed a change. I had been, at one time or another, a stock market research analyst, an institutional salesman, an investment banker and a founder of a small broker/investment banking company. After leaving that business I started, with one partner, Ben Huston, an investment partnership typically called a hedge fund.

As luck would have it, shortly after retiring, my long-time friend Lesley Lavack told me about a summer abroad course she was going to attend at Oxford University and she advised me to come as well. These programs are designed for undergraduates but some alumni often attend. It sounded pretty cool to me. It was a stimulating and fun 5 weeks as a student again after so many years in the work world and it ignited my interest in studying . My educational background had been in Mathematics but I was now interested in the Humanities. I started auditing classes at Bay Area universities with my first one at Berkeley followed by several at the University of San Francisco and finally quite a few at Stanford. How that was possible is a whole other story!

Years into this new mode of life, I started writing poetry for fun. Again, as luck would have it, my friend Andy Luce suggested I start a blog for my poetry and he set it up for me. That was towards the end of 2012. I write spontaneously and follow up with some editing. The blog steered itself in a philosophical direction although the work also contains some satire and some political poems. I am not prolific and only publish about 2 per month. They are generally short and I hope pithy. This style is probably due to my Math background where elegance and conciseness are prized over length.

The two big changes in my life since leaving the work world are my writing and even more importantly an explosion in the number of fantastic friendships I have been privileged to form. My more recent friends come from many walks of life including non financial businesses, academia, the dance world, and the art world. When you work 10 hours a day you gravitate towards friends in your own industry.

The poems are in the order published starting with the latest and working backwards to the first. The only exception is the first poem whose title is the same as this book. Since it deals with the wonder and limitations of language, it seemed appropriate to lead with it. I hope you enjoy reading them.

—Gary Ross

CONTENTS

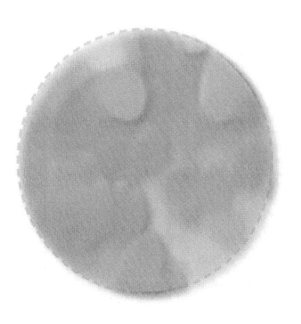

Sublime Confinement

words tumble down

like snowflakes in the mind

metaphors piling upon metaphors

mustering into drifts blown away

melted back to the void

Is I the first metaphor

Is We the second

can we ponder without words

chained to language

as we are

our secret labyrinth

prison and escape

Pillars Of Life

comprehending

connecting

creating

compassion

hold on to the extraordinary

ordinary will take care

of itself

DOUBLE BIND

conscious thinking
each day
drowns out wondering
of the subconscious
the major part
of our mind

lovely possible moments
have been lost

subconscious thinking
each night
supplants ordered thought
freeing us from
preformed ideas
rejecting others
that might make more sense

lovely possible moments
have been lost

Trial By Experience

sometimes

we choose a hard road

sometimes

it chooses us

the measure of our mettle

is tested psychologically

as knights of yore

were tested physically

stick to your guiding compass

in each situation

you find yourself in

it may or may not

work out as hoped

but best you can do

WHAT'S UP DOC

squares round to circles

imponderables dance

all around us

terrible morphs to tolerable

all is in flux

making us fluxom

false sense of certainty

has flown the coop

driving some into

fatal fearful ideologies

other to wide-eyed wisdom

no simple answers

in this chaotic maelstrom

THERAPY

forget the past

live in presence

forge your future

Reckless Sapiens

we clubbed our way

to the top of the pyramid

what a powerful species

are we

big brains

small minds

is overpopulation a problem

is aggression a problem

or lack of compassion

moving to Mars

isn't a solution

just spreading

problems elsewhere

as a short term oriented
species

we are ill equipped

to resolve planetary stress

probably

probably not

depends on our choices

MALICIOUS MONKEY

hate inspired

by religion

by race

by ideology

is no new news

tribalism is a core aspect

of our sorry malicious state

hard to break away

from our

cultural history

ATTACHMENTS

to family

friends and lovers

work and activities

ideology and religion

our gravities

they are

but our attachments

do produce

love

energy

exhilaration

empathy and passion

leading to

inspiration and creativity

sticking to someone

or something

seems rather important

we are like water

tumbling over a ledge

without any scoring

clinging

desperately

to the wall

of our connections

STIFF UPPER LIP

like a dam

we must all

hold back

in our case

emotional

overreaction

to stress

preserving decorum

obeying unwritten

rules of the road

easier to burst forth

pour out our anger

sink in frustration

stirring up the pot

but it might boil over

burning our own hands

best to use the spillways

Ruly/Unruly

the first rule of love
Be Ruled By Love

the second rule
Beware The First Rule

Bytesize

the unemployment rate

of words

has been rising

but no one cares

thin vocabulary

like emaciated models

commands our attention

subtle complex wording

hides real truth

who needs erudition

images are more compelling

for many

words are for old fogies

text me baby

instasnap me baby

twit us all

what of importance

could possibly be lost

The Way We are Now

the center has fallen

extremes are unleashed

woe to reason when

demagogues rule

to the detriment of all

intolerance

usually simmering

now heats up

takes front stage

speech from all sides

has been sidelined

by biases

HAIL TO THE CHIEF

trumperie

tromperie

bellicosity

we bought it

what to do now?

twitterer-in-chief

let us pray

for relief

WHEEL OF FORTUNE

betimes you think

counterfactual possibilities

aspirations all fulfilled

dangers all engaged

to your benefit

the raw truth

is less audacious

but still fulfilling

we are always more

and always less

than our dreams

PETERPAN

the past is the shadow

following and leading

us around

to our future

its parchment

so well worn

still has sprightliness

in its heels

kicking us along

our most uncertain journey

to a destination that

perhaps is only known

to It

Mirrored

old young

jealousy admiration

love love

each teaches

each learns

growth sustains

till death do us part

Singularities

no coupling here
only singularities

a wind blows
from the valley
mountains are mute

below begets above
cold becomes warm
opposites exchange
their dark humor
mobius we are

Divided Mind

waking up

going to sleep

daily

nightly

each minute

each hour

involvement with

detachment from

external reality

conjoined twins

constantly competing

for attention

Synthesis

untroubled Being

an unattainable goal

except for dogs

consciousness creates

mind earthquakes

doubts of the soul

hesitation of hearts

thinking has its biases

logic its limitations

overthinking does too

the great balancing act

must go on

inside our heads

Happiness

no IV available

infection from others

unlikely

it has to come

from the inside

a state of being

beyond circumstances

Bumpy Roads

guess what

Buddha was right

pain and suffering

surround us

periodic for some

permanent for others

two car garages

unlimited data plans

big bank balances

are not enough

fortitude

joyfulness

lovingness

kindness

sure do help

Who What Why

we are the
heights of creativity
we are the
depths of depravity

in search of
self justification
or meaning
sometimes sought
via the pursuit of
an all encompassing
ideological dream state
invariably to disappoint

we are
mostly muddling
through the middle
mildly rippling
whatever wave
of harmony or dystopia
is in fashion

why can't we just deal
with the world as it is
try to make
small improvements
within our orbit of possibilities
accepting the frailty
of our conditional fate

the same old tune
is always playing
self interest
competing
with empathy

POLITRICKERY

the left wing is intolerant

the right wing is intolerant

can someone please

clip their wings

HEALING

magical music

makes me happy

simple but serious

complex but soothing

like me I am

transported to the

island of pure being

no doubts

no fears

just a few tears

GROUNDING

as a bird flies

so do our dreams

soaring in spite of

our gravity

too close to

the searing sun

of impracticality

one must not go

can one toe

tied to the ground

lift one up

in deed it can

AGENCY

In The Land Of Ican

Imagination was valued

Creativity was revered

Success was admired

Truth embraced

and

Wisdom treasured

In The Land Of Youcan

imagination is repressed

creativity is stifled

success leads to jealousy

lies abound

and

wisdom is trashed

POSSIBLITIES

hope transgresses despair

dreams can trump defeat

will can change

your outcome

outcomes can change

worlds around you

worlds around you

can bring relief

from temporality

LIFE SCORE

energetic positive engagement

X

your age

=

your life score

Lessons

those who remember history

are usually condemned to relive it

HOLY SMOKES—HOLY GHOSTS

in the beginning

God was bored

immutability was not

all it had been

made out to be

A Big Bang was needed

somewhat frustrated

gazillions of years later

with continued predictability

in its creation

God

dreamed up Man

what a job man has done

all is mutable Now

all is malleable Now

watch out universe

the virus might spread !

OLD/YOUNG

testament to

ripened vines

sweet nectar

shedding light

on sorrows and joys

of the past

present is now compelling

no longer dragged down

by failures of the past

or fears of the future

is hope diminished

are new journeys possible

set as we are in old ways

all depends on you

the world of you Now

can be

your new Youth

Death

end time

for I for me

subject no more

object of sorrow

or delight

or derision

was was

not is is

is all of fate

in one verb

Eco

acidize the oceans

pollute the rivers

carbonize the air

terrorize the earth

what else can we do

to earn the distinction

of being crafted

in God's image

MYRIAD ROLES

the art of Being

being about connecting

has many faces

spouse sibling

lover partner

father friend

creator worker

mentor

sparking

one hell of a good time

is a great role too

GORDIAN

past present future

continuous contention

red hot ingot

hammered out by

whom

what will will do

to alter outcomes

are we prisoners of our past

are we creators of our future

spun as we are

around the vortex

of infinity

or nothingness

WOOF WOOF

exotic dream
something to
look forward to
God and Afterlife

as if this gift
of life itself
were not enough

complaining species
we are
never content
never fulfilled

ever heard complaints
from your dog
can they teach us
something important

Vulnerability

In Memory Of A Friend

all that shit

all that shrapnel

descending on us

like comic cosmic rays

mocking our self sufficiency

our lack of real power

confined

as we are

to such a small planck

Of Space/Time

ORDINARY INTERUPTED

as I crossed

an intersection today

grief rudely interrupted me

a woman in her griefmobile

was sobbing at the steering wheel

windows rolled up

I could not hear

what had happened to her

on this all too

ordinary day

I will never

know the cause

but I felt the pain

which strikes like lightning

on all of us some day

Life's Choices

optimism pessimism realism

so many isms wanting attention

what to suckle now

what to be suckled by

and the answer is- Da Da Da

be optimistic about your world

be pessimistic about global issues

pray for reason to prevail

if all else fails

have a lot of fun

do it anyway!!

Devotion

tears of war

tear peoples apart

tears of war

tie people together

adherents of faith

blind people together

adherents of faith

break peoples apart

INEQUALITY

beauty smarts
education efforts
sociability connections
luck and choices
income and wealth

damned DNA
damned environment
seems so unfair
if life did not
soar to your dreams
just wait

one day we may
engineer our offspring
equal in all ways
ban two sidedness
outlaw luck
restore uniformity
is that not Utopia

TROMPE L'ESPRIT

narrative imperative

mind's manifesto

call for clarity

in a muddy world

flight to safety

shaping the misshapen

to order chaos

begin muddle end

PERFECT PORTAL

Oh Beauty

you do teach me

I see in thee

so many versions of the world

multitudinous perspectives

stories and emotions

working on me

like plasticine

LOVE'S DREAM

there is a beacon

beckoning him

from afar to dear

guiding and directing him

to you

what wonders await this searcher

on this ocean of life

that lifts his wandering soul

can fulfillment rival dreams

so perfect

so unblemished

fantasies so fantastic

to be believable

but perhaps

imperfection is the real

Perfection

West-East

logos swaddles wisdom

action suckles wisdom

action seeks wisdom

contemplation is wisdom

light matter or dark matter

You choose

Perishing

right time

wrong time

ripe fruit

well spent

honeycombed memories

joys and sorrows

solitude's sanctuary

sweet connections

success setback

steep paths

sharp declines

mere mortals

we are

waxing and waning

accepting

Philosophical Therapy

finitude	transcendence
solitude	connections
anxiety	presence
boredom	purpose
contemplation	experiences
death	humor
inexplicability	ejaculation

IDENTITY

are you

the cats meow

fit as a fiddle

happy as a lark

on a lark

contented as a cow

left to its deVices

miserable as misers

angry as a hornets nest

lonely as a wondering soul

wandering throughout the above

quiet as a church mouse

carted before the horse

happy as a clambake

bull in a china shop

impatient as a nun

chasing after God

persistent as woodpeckers

enthusiastic as dogs

LIFESPAN

it's all darkness

it's all light

shadows fill in slowly

mind grows

body declines

canvas gets graver

grayer and greater

humor not lost

just escalated

it's the end

it's all darkness

SELF REVEALING

friendship is its own explanation

it requires none

though time itself should mock

friendship endures

a tribute and a pledge

bringing wealth

to its bearers

CHOICES

three great beauties

three ugly masters

vying for submission

experience reflection dreams

present past futures

choose your elixir

but keep somewhat

grounded in presence

What Seduction Means

whispering willows

warn wanderers

wild wily weekends

with lovers

sprout senselessly

snaring salubrious

otherwise sensible sojourners

molding them

mocking them

making magical music

but be aware

pleasure can pain

New Careening

a man was crawling

in his space

projectile to nowhere

where is somewhere?

it's not Plastics anymore

we've graduated to connectedness

Apple Google Facebook

Twitter we are

Snap to

the new plastic

Co Dependency

Night opens up my eyes

day ushers in monotony

night makes me laugh and cry

Day creates the space for night

Shoals

I was crossing an ocean in my mind

fending off frightful waves

steering clear of many shoals

only to realize

those shoals are stepping stones

leading to

humility and wisdom

Internal Success

Honesty

Hunger for Life

Lovingness

Self Awareness

Compassion

Humor

Humility

Forgiveness

EXTERNAL SUCCESS

talent perseverance

salesmanship

amiability toughness

inheritance

connections

deception

manipulation

ruthlessness

criminality

Many possible combinations of Good & Bad

Pacifiers

Politicians get elected

by making unreasonable promises

to an unreasoning public

Democracy's Achilles heel

is revealing itself now

Success destroys from within

FRENEMY

Ego is your best friend
when inspiring you
Ego is your worst friend
when it gets bruised

INTUITION

quest for the right questions

search for the solveable

has been the foundation

but the unsolvable

yet knowable is

the key to unlock

the riddle of

a more comlex

post Parmenidean world

DRAMA

when things are tough

just remember

without drama

there would be no need

for Shakespeare

TWILIGHT OF THE HUMANS

Whisper Whisper

Talk   Talk

Shout Shout

about a

change in consciousness

about

our place in Nature

our responsibilities to Nature

our responsibilities to Ourselves

legacies we are creating

Overpopulation/Pollution

Climate Change

Species Extinction

Mercury Rising

Plastic Detritus

Does this sound like intelligent design

Visual Rendering

abstract art is the source code

of fluid pre-formed possibilities

realism is one static rendered finale

we live now in

the fluid world

Green Grass/Grey Grass

We live in a cauldron

of wished for tales

hungering for the lives

we could have had

but one Epitaph is all we shall have

We live in a cauldron of feared for tales

fleeing from the lives we could have had

so pleased with our short epitaph

Owed to a Kettle

Oh ketel oh ketel

Oh Ketel One ™

It sure doesn't take you very long

to boil away the day and

brew up delight in the night!

CAREERS

Philosophers

they charge like a posse of Don Quixotes
armed with the lance of reason
aiming to pierce the heart
of contingency and irrationality
hoping to restore Certainty
to its former supreme position
reality merely bats its eyelashes and rolls on.

Politicians

they swarm like a hive of locusts
armed with the lance of power
promising the impossible while
devouring the public purse
stinging all in their way
as they charge for re election
public service has morphed into self service

PROSTITUTES

unarmed as they are

they humble themselves

to give joy to others

ridiculed often by those they serve

a short career is in store for them

all they have to give

is their fleeting beauty

Mourning

I miss you during the day and I miss you during the
night

the future of no new experiences together has created a
black hole inside of me

it grows and contracts as the world without you flickers
on and off

I know Time's plan to annihilate our past together

But I won't let you completely dissolve inside of me

You did after all reconnect me to the best part of myself

Mantras On The Move

1953- put your shoulder to the wheel

Today- at no cost to you

1953- whats good for General Motors is good for America

Now- whats good for the Generals is good

La Meillure Partie

La meillure partie qui

se passe sous la fenetre de nos ames

c'est la creativite joint a

l'amour de la vie

AGING

A man looked in the mirror

aging but ageless

joy judicious but deeper

friends more important

more stimulating

age not wasted on the old after all

while the drums quietly beat your demise

trumpets celebrate your arrival

into wisdom and forgiveness

TO BE OR NOT TO BE

Your actions and your inactions are key drivers of
your fate, except when rare Black Swan events trump
everything. For the choices YOU make, you should
struggle for connectedness and creativity, hoping for
the best- which sometimes turns out to be the worst, at
least, in the short term. Of course, you can't know the
outcomes of your choices in advance – that would make
the whole thing silly. The contest between change and
stasis must always exist and if either of them totally
dominates –what a scary or boring life it would be.
Obstacles can purify us, and taking actions that over-
come them does provide the temporary calm we all
strive for but can never live with for too long.

HUBRIS 2

if man is the measure of all things

made-to-measure is the only fashion

in the universe

Time/Temps

Stop! Watch!

listen and learn

the canvas and cadence

of ours flashing by

Present! Past!

whatwhenwhy

Arrêtez! Regardez!

écoutez et apprennez

le cour et cadence

de n'heures qui s'envolent

Présent! Passé!

quiquandquoi

ENLIGHTENMENT TO BLIGHTENMENT

Social Contract........21st C Self Serving Politicians

Science....................Nukes, CO2

Medicine......................Overpopulation

Capitalism...........Wealth........Obesity

Hope..................................Lemmings

TWINS

JOY

most have some

a few a lot

gather it close

one great day subdues

ten difficult ones

like armour in the past

PAIN

we all carry

some around

how to cope

bury it

suffer through it

use it to another end

best to transcend

Responsibility

stand on your own shoulders

the other ones are occuppied

Why Not

Gifts from Bacchus

cozy nights with friends

unclogged drain of modern mantra

restoring unversed conversation to
sooth rough spots—the wounds of Order.

We feel younger—the night grows older

the vine of our emotions—glad and sad

serves up its fruit of love

I-You You-I

dance with me—your mind

For Tonight is thine.

Owed To Mari Wanna?

High-why not

a can opener and a rose

blooming consciousness

holding forth on secrets

shocking us into laughter

revelations without religion.

here the connected unconnected notes are

uncorked and quaffed to quench the greatest thirst of all

until a flute of peaceful tranquility descends

Dance with me—my mind

No morrow shall undermine

COMPLEXITY

Linear thinking

doesn't solve problems

in a quadratic world

if only

politicians and generals

could learn that

HUBRIS

Alexander tried and failed

Rome did swell

till waves overran it

not so Great Britain picked up

the folly

only to fumble

last in line to square the circle

not so holy America

succumbed to the mantra of power

Exceptional-Yes

Unexceptional-Yes

What's new

Loss

though death does stalk us

and those we love

each and every day

like a sly fox

waiting to devour

the thin fabric of our happiness

and all that we have and all that we are

is asunder in time

never the less

to honor those taken from ourselves

and give meaning to our ongoing lives

we must try our hardest

to brave that fox and transcend our finiteness

by living a beautiful, loving, and creative existence

Two Markets

have you ever noticed how few

funeral homes there are

even though so deeply $$$ consecrated.

supermarkets on the other hand are everywhere

they only deal in tender recent vintage slaughter

THE CIRCLE

Begin End

curious circle of helplessness

can't run from the past

can't a void the future

Live in the middle

where illusions provide some relief from

the burden of consciousness.

DIFFERENT STROKES

One mink stole

steals a woman's soul

One whiff of Power

turns a man's sour

GOD

God is great

but she has been taking

an awe fully long vacation

if God existed

it wouldn't care

about your faith

just your actions

THE YOKE IS ON US

on this perilous journey in Time

sandwiched as we are

somewhere between cockroaches and black holes

hammed in on all sides by a

gigantic joke called the Universe

the point of which is known only to

Madmen and Saints-

It seems that Great Illusions win out

Because all else fails!

THE MEANING OF NO MEANING

Such a dazzling and beautiful morning in the
   countryside is it
My wise companion knows what a special day it is
Dew soaks the deck and table
While it kisses the grass and flowers
The heat will end all that very soon- but for now
I feast my eyes, drink hot coffee and pull up the
   umbrella to see more clearly
My mind wanders while I stroke my never-in-doubt
   and share some of my toast
I guess you could call it breaking bread

The oleanders are shimmering colorfully with
   expectation
But the rock roses are still asleep
Their makeup is waiting for next month when they
   will briefly overshadow the rest of the garden
It is getting warmer already and the shadows are
   growing smaller-foreshadowing an end of sorts

The barking tells me that it's time for a walk
I thought I loved this special morning
But just watch him
It's a one of a kind day for him- just like all the others
The internet tells me there is more of the same in store

The morning has given way to a soporific afternoon
I'm at the pool pretending to read- things don't
    quite look the same anymore
My know-it-all is curled up peacefully

The morning I now realize is dead
What was its meaning, what was its purpose?
The friendly bark tells me that it's time to move on
You can't hold the past in your hands
The past can't hold you in its grip
Nevertheless, it was a beautiful morning

The Web Of life

throughout our lives
unknown to us
a web is being spun
for good or for ill
we are carried along
quite unconscious of what it is and what is
happening all around us
caught up as we are
in our own particular worlds
the blind folders of which
can never be removed

once in a while fate gives us a special gift – someone
to connect with, laugh with and eventually to love
just the reverse of romantic love
where the love starts first.
they are gifts from the gods
these angels who tread near our souls
bending our consciousness
like the sun that draws flowers to its life giving rays

Aiming High

breaking good
is The challenge
not so easy as you think
you being a prisoner
of your desires , self interest
and
cultural imperatives

aiming for a higher
state of Being
contradicts human nature
but you must bend
nature to your will
liberating your soul
helping others
freeing your mind
from cultural imperatives
and
DNA dispositions

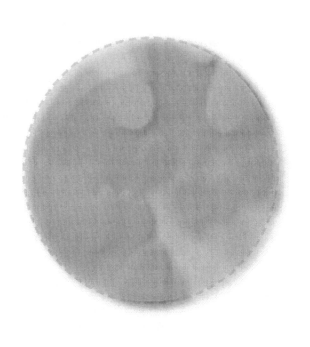

ABOUT THE AUTHOR

Gary Ross grew up in Toronto, Canada. At the University of Toronto he studied Mathematics and after graduating he started a career in Finance, first in Toronto, and subsequently in New York where he worked on Wall Street. He moved to San Francisco permanently in 1991 where he, along with two former associates, started an investment company. In 2004 he retired and began auditing classes in the Humanities, primarily in Literature and Philosophy, at Bay Area Universities. In 2013 he began writing philosophical poetry which he published on a blog. This volume contains most of that work. He has one daughter who lives in Los Angeles.

81463818R00106

Made in the USA
San Bernardino, CA
07 July 2018